OVERCOMING EVIL WITH GOOD

OVERCOMING EVIL WITH GOOD

JOSEPH M. STOWELL

MOODY PRESS

CHICAGO

ISBN: 0-8024-4699-X

1 3 5 7 9 10 8 6 4 2

Printed in the United States of America

Mother Teresa was the featured speaker at the February 1994 National Prayer Breakfast in Washington, D.C. With President Bill Clinton, his wife, Hillary, and the Gores in attendance, she stood fearlessly at the podium, and in the context of her speech proclaimed: "I feel that the greatest destroyer of peace today is abortion, because it is war against the child, a direct killing of the innocent child, murder by the mother herself. . . . By abortion the mother does not learn to love, but kills even her own child to solve her problems. And by abortion the father is told that he does not have to take any responsibility at all for the child he has brought into the world. That father is likely to put other women into the same trouble. So abortion just leads to more abortion. Any country that accepts abortion is not teaching its people to love, but to use violence to get what they want. This is why the greatest destroyer of love and peace is abortion."[1]

The crowd rose to its feet in thunderous applause as the Clintons and Gores remained uneasily seated, waiting for the program to continue.

Interestingly, as President Clinton began his address to the group, he responded, "It's hard to argue with a life so well lived."

It was a strategic moment. This aged, stooped woman who had given herself to helping less fortunate people had now, with no political power or clout, built a platform with her life that disarmingly caught the attention of one of the most influential advocates of abortion.

The moment is noteworthy for those of us who are concerned about the drift toward godlessness in our society—unusual because we have so few moments of victory in our battle against the encroaching paganism of our day. It was a ray of hope in a seemingly hopeless, dark night for Christians; a skirmish won on a battlefield where victories have been scarce. It was significant because it was a moment of triumph: triumph for what is right, not won by political lobbying or leverage but rather by the power of a life lived in such a way that it had indisputable credibility and power.

Although I have some significant theological differences with Mother Teresa, it cannot be denied that she has dedicated her life to the kind of works that moved a mountain that morning in Washington, D.C.

The dynamic at that breakfast stands as a model of what it will take if we are to catch the attention of a shamelessly sinful society and fulfill our mandate not to be overcome with evil but to overcome evil with good (Romans 12:21). It is a model of what it takes to cultivate a curiosity in others that will open hearts to the life-changing message of Christ.

Overcomers

The Armitage Baptist Church is one of the leading evangelical churches in the city of Chicago. It is positioned in the heart of one of our toughest neighborhoods and is led by a second-generation city pastor. On the first anniversary of the murder of Dr. David Gunn, an abortion clinic doctor in Florida, pro-abortion activists around the country decided to commemorate the moment with what they called a Night of Resistance. This Night of Resistance would comprise demonstrations to make a distinct point for their cause and profile Christians as radical, murderous elements of society.

Of all the places that they could have chosen to demonstrate in Chicago, they selected Armitage Baptist Church. I was a guest speaker there the Sunday night before the demonstration. It was clear that brothers and sisters in that church felt concern. Yet they were courageously ready to proceed with their prayer meeting and, in fact, to use it as an opportunity for massive prayer that the cause of Christ might prevail.

For years the members of Armitage Baptist Church have patiently and persistently established a beachhead for God by submitting the agenda and program of their church to the authority of Christ. The members have reached their culturally diverse Chicago neighborhood by showing hospitality to all who live there. The church addresses neighborhood needs through a variety of ministries that demonstrate the kind of works that are reflective of an unhindered, unqualified submission to the lordship of Christ.

Members have unashamedly, yet compassionately, stood for righteousness against the powerful influences of gay activism and the agendas of the abortionists that are so influential in neighborhoods such as theirs. As they prayerfully prepared to face the militant gay and abortion groups of Chicago that had targeted Armitage for their demonstration, I detected an unusual sense of calm and confidence. This would be a rather unsettling event for any church, but an especially unsettling prospect for a church located in such a volatile gang-ridden neighborhood.

A couple of weeks later, while returning from a trip, I picked up the airplane copy of *U.S. News & World Report*. As I leisurely thumbed through the magazine, the headline in John Leo's column, "On Society," caught my attention. The headline read, "An Anti-antiabortion Rally." Knowing what the media usually does to people like us in contexts like this, I braced myself to take another cultural hit at our stand. To my surprise the reporter was discussing the incident at Armitage. He wrote,

> Demonstrators were supposed to bring whistles and other noise-makers to drown out church services. The Women's Action Coalition planned to bring its "drum corps." Flyers posted around town to draw a major crowd urged demonstrators to "Dress to shock *and/or impress*, come in costume and show your rage." . . . The sponsors included Queer Nation, an anarchist youth group, Sister Serpents (an underground women's collective), and the National Committee to Free Puerto Rican POWs and Political Prisoners. A few demonstrators wore patches that said "Feminist Witch" and "Support Vaginal Pride" . . . The church was expecting trouble . . .

Leo went on to say,

The most common chant was "Racist, sexist, antigay/ Born-again bigots, go away." The "racist" charge is particularly weird: The Armitage congregation is roughly 30 percent black, 30 percent Hispanic and 40 percent white. The security force on the steps seemed about half Hispanic. The church is in the Logan Square area, a neighborhood mixed by class and race, maybe 60 percent Hispanic, 25 percent white, and 15 percent black. For "born-again bigots," the congregation has made an unusually successful effort to cut across racial lines.

I wanted to stand on my airplane seat, wave the article for everyone to see, and shout Amen and Amen! . . . Leo continued,

While the crowd chanted about racism, a group of young black men showed up wearing long red jackets that said "SHS Security." They were from a South Side black Baptist church, the Sweet Holy Spirit, and had come to protect a fellow evangelical church.

Somewhat confused, the woman with the bullhorn tried to lead the crowd in singing "Little Boxes," a song about suburban conformity popularized by Pete Seeger in the 1960s. It was, without a doubt, the least appropriate song anyone could have sung about this diverse urban congregation.

Next, five yellow buses rolled up and a seemingly endless stream of people poured out. . . . They were evangelicals from a second South Side church, mostly black families, showing up for the service. More than a thousand people were now in the church.

The security men had been singing all along, picking fast-paced music that almost matched the volume of the demonstrators. Now, they gave way to a choir of black kids. The demonstrators were done for. The kids were too good and too loud.[2]

Later I talked with Charles Lyons, the pastor of the Armitage church. He added a P.S. to the article. For days before the demonstration, demonstrators had canvassed every home in the neighborhood with leaflets inviting individuals to come and join the demonstration. In a neighborhood which is prone to positive perspectives on both the gay and abortion issues, one might have expected a pretty good turnout. But Pastor Lyons noted that not one neighbor joined the demonstration. I asked him why. He replied that the neighbors have come to know that Armitage Baptist Church cares for them and is concerned about their needs. When the Chicago school system could not open for several days in the fall of 1993 due to budget problems, the schoolteachers who attended his church volunteered their time and opened up an alternate school in their building for the neighborhood children.

Their good works not only silenced a powerful group of adversaries but created a neighborhood beachhead that even the most hostile opponents could not erode—a triumph won by the compelling power of lives well lived.

Concerned Christians

I don't know that I've met a serious Christian who isn't deeply concerned with the dramatic shift in the American culture. We're concerned for ourselves, for our children, for our grandchildren, and for the cause of the gospel. Formerly the moral authority of God's Word was the base for both societal life and law, yet now God's law and biblical morality are not only ignored but often ridiculed. As Arnold Toynbee has observed, "We are the first generation of man to try to build a society without a moral reference point."

This loss has led to massive efforts by Christians and Christian organizations to regain what we have lost and to take our country back to a time when we felt more safe, stable, and secure. We miss that time when Christians and Christianity were part and parcel of the mainstream in

America. For the vast majority of Christians, this desire to reclaim our culture is interpreted in terms of regaining the reins of political power. Individual Christians, churches, and nationally organized coalitions of influential leaders are leading the charge to reclaim America. The passion among some approaches a frenzied pitch. There seem to be few things we would not sacrifice in terms of time, energy, money, and talk to get our country back.

All of us would agree that it is important to hold our government accountable for righteousness. As citizens we should care about values that reflect biblical morality. It is our responsibility to use the leverage we have in terms of voting, running for office, and putting godly people on the school boards and in state houses and in Washington, D.C. I personally celebrate the efforts in these arenas and affirm those who keep us informed and enable us to respond intelligently.

But we have to ask whether the primary agenda of the church is to reclaim the American culture. To even the casual observer it would appear that Christianity and politics are not only comfortable bedfellows but that Christians have made political activism a vital part of their Christian expression.

First Things First

If we are not careful we may find that we have developed a deeper passion for the politics of the here and now than for the eternal destiny of lost souls. In fact, it is possible for our political agendas to override our capacity to reach the lost. We disenfranchise ourselves from those who need Christ on the other end of the political spectrum with our often hostile rhetoric and by posturing ourselves as their enemies. In so doing we mix the liberating message of Jesus Christ with political notions that polarize their hearts from Christ and His redemption. As deeply as we value a return to a morally safe America, we have to ask if we value that more highly than the weight of eternity on anyone's soul, and in particular on the souls of our political adversaries.

It is not a matter of one or the other. It is a matter of which holds the highest value; of which will be the point of our primary passion and provide the grid through which all of our political activism is passed. I personally pray for, hope for, and vote for a safer, more moral America. But the gospel must hold the upper hand. *Spiritual* triumph is our calling. The worst that could happen is not that we "lose America" but that we lose or even diminish our platform to reach all Americans with the life-changing message of Christ.

Reality Check

Let us say that in all our financial contributions, efforts, and energy we succeed in bringing America back to its moral roots. Several important realities would have to be kept in mind. First, given the fact that we live in a democracy, it will always be a *slippery* victory in terms of its longevity. It really is only good until the next election, and since it didn't come through conversion but through ballots, it more probably was based on pragmatic choices rather than spiritual commitment.

We would have to remember as well that political victories are always *secondary* in terms of a biblical worldview. While reclamation of our culture may help keep our world safe and stable and create an environment into which the gospel can flow more freely, a political triumph is not effective in terms of the mission that Christ gave to the church to go into all the world and preach the gospel. God has called us not to save America, but to save Americans. Changing America really is a matter of changing one American at a time, regardless of the political environment. Carl Henry notes for us, "If we seek to capture men's minds, and struggle for just social structures, yet neglect the evangelization of the earth, we shall fail our generation where it needs help most of all."[3]

If we succeed in returning America to its Judeo-Christian foundations through political clout, America will be more safe, stable, and sane, but this would be a *shallow* victory. As wonderful as a reclaimed America would be, Americans would not be committed to biblical values because of an unwavering commitment to Christ and His truth. Ravi Zacharias notes, "If we succeed in making America more moral, then what we will have is more lost moral Americans." In *Pilgrim's Progress*, Pilgrim gets sidetracked into a layover in the village of Morality where all is morally correct. He finds, however, that morality without the cross is unable to alleviate his burden of sin.

In addition, political triumph is a *seductive* pursuit. It tempts us to shift our eyes away from the focus of the church, a primary concern not only for the lost but also for the growth and development of our own lives in Jesus Christ. Many of us can identify with the woman who approached me recently before a meeting and related that for the last two years she had been so deeply involved in political causes that she had neglected her growth in Christ as well as her commitments to her local church in terms of both time and giving. She had even come to see those on the other side of the political fence as enemies rather than ones for whom Christ died. She admitted that during this time her intimacy with Christ had dimmed. She had recently been convicted about how quickly her political adrenaline had eclipsed her passion for the lost souls of her enemies and for things of Christ and eternity.[4]

It is far more comfortable for us to believe that we are doing our Christian duty by marching, politicking, protesting, and supporting groups that do than it is for us to keep focused on the most important task of our faith—glorifying Him through personal growth into the likeness of Christ and a commitment to the eternal destinies of friends and neighbors. Our lives have the capacity for only so many things in a particular segment of time. Given a choice, we'll often opt for the advancement of causes rather than the development of character in our walk with Christ. When that happens, we begin to interpret authentic Christianity as a commitment to a given cause instead of a calling to Christ and His church. That may be why many of our political endeavors are tainted with godless attitudes, actions, and reactions; why the church seems to be more angry over politics than in anguish over lost souls.

I find myself wondering if we have supposed that it is the government's responsibility to advance righteousness and be the steward, upholder, promoter, and protector of biblical truth and values. Scripture assigns to government the responsibilities of safety, stability, peace, and justice (1 Timothy 2:2; Romans 13:1–5). Yet we give the impression that we feel betrayed by our government because it is no longer an advocate for truth and righteousness. These are the responsibilities of the church, not the government. We need to remind ourselves that the passages of Scripture on the role of government were written to Christians living in a pagan environment far worse than ours, about leaders and political systems more ruthless than ours. Actually, as American Christians we have lived in an unusual season of history: We've had a government that, although ruled for the most part by those who were not authentically Christian, was built on the fundamental tenets of our biblical heritage. Most Christians through the ages have lived under hostile, oppressive, pagan governmental systems. And, quite frankly, Christians have often done their best in those environments.

It was to Christians in such an environment that Paul delineated our responsibility toward government. We are to honor those in authority over us, pray for them, and pay our taxes. Thankfully, Scripture doesn't say that we have to vote for them; but since they are ultimately placed in authority by God's decree we are commanded to give them due respect (Romans 13:1, 5–7). This biblical perspective recognizes God's sovereign oversight, realigns our attitudes, and releases us to get on with the business of carrying the torch of His redemptive power.

I wonder if our natural aversion to suffering may be at play in our passion to regain politically what we have lost? Having lived in such a comfortable, compatible, and spiritually convenient environment, could it be that we resist the thought of facing what legions of our forefathers faced with courage and strength: living in an inhospitable environment that is hostile to our values and that inflicts measures of discomfort on us for clinging to what we hold dear? The hymn writer Isaac Watts wrote some rather probing questions:

Am I a soldier of the cross,
A follower of the Lamb,
And shall I fear to own His cause,
Or blush to speak His name?

Must I be carried to the skies
On flowery beds of ease,
While others fought to win the prize,
And sailed through bloody seas?

Are there no foes for me to face?
Must I not stem the flood?
Is this vile world a friend to grace,
To help me on to God?

Sure, I must fight, if I would reign;
Increase my courage, Lord;
I'll bear the toil, endure the pain,
Supported by Thy Word.

God does not expect us to be masochistic and hope for suffering. But if He calls us to suffer at the hands of a hostile culture in the course of our non-negotiated commitment to His values and to the cause of the gospel, then we need to be ready to do it graciously, without being intimidated.

Finally, a primary focus on political triumph is at best *short-sighted*. Living in oppressive times always raises interest in trying to manage the environment to our benefit, to bring about better times. It is interesting that some of the most committed people this world has ever known, the disciples, constantly longed that Christ might in their lifetime restore the kingdom to Israel. They expected that Jesus Christ had come to overthrow the oppressive Roman regime that was so foreign to the values and legacy of Judaism, to establish His kingdom on earth where He would rule and righteousness would reign. Their impulses were really not much different from our impulses today, except that we don't expect Christ to come to America to overthrow our political oppression . . . though we would be delighted if some messianic type of person would occupy the Oval Office in Washington, D.C., someday soon. Yet revival has never been spawned by political victory. The battles of the kingdom are fought on different soil.

Although it was within Christ's power to conquer the political systems of His day, and although Satan offered Him the "kingdoms of the world, and their glory" (Matthew 4:8), He resisted the temptation and instead focused on spiritual, eternal triumph in terms of the defeat of sin, death, and hell at the Cross and through an empty grave.

Upon His resurrection, the disciples no doubt were thinking that since He had so clearly verified His right to rule through His resurrection, this would be the time when He would overthrow the political regime and take them back to better days like the "good old days" when the Jews were under their own rule. In Acts 1, after Christ's resurrection and just before He ascended into heaven, they asked Him again, "Lord, is it at this time You are restoring the kingdom to Israel?" He said to them, "It is not for you to know times or epochs which the Father has fixed by His own authority; but you shall receive power when the Holy Spirit has come upon you; and you shall be My witnesses both in Jerusalem, and in all Judea and Samaria, and even to the remotest part of the earth" (Acts 1:6–8).

It's not that there isn't a kingdom to come. We are assured of the eternal reality known as heaven. But in Christ's final interaction with the disciples about their compelling, seemingly all-consuming desire for political triumph and release from oppression, we cannot overlook the fact that He deferred their legitimate hope for a compatible and godly government and sent them out to win people to populate eternity. For Christ the compelling issue was always—and still is—the work of the Cross, not the assumption of the crown. That must be our primary compulsion as well.

What Then?

At this point it would be easy to assume that we should forget about the deepening decadence of our society and simply evangelize. That's not my point. God expects us to hold our culture accountable for righteousness. With compassion and without intimidation, we need to do all that is within our means to check the drift and hopefully restore a measure of safety and stability through a return to the tested and proven principles of our Judeo-Christian heritage. But political triumph cannot eclipse the more important reason for our existence on this earth, and that is redemptive, eternal triumph.

Quite frankly, as I attempt to balance the priority of eternal gain over temporal gain, I find myself recoiling at the thought that we might lose America if we don't pour the majority of our efforts down the chute of political leverage. Yet, my heart is steadied and my mind is satisfied when I contemplate God's sovereignty. For reasons best known to God, in His sovereign intentions regarding the flow of history, He may permit America to move toward a deepening paganism. In fact, revival has often been staged on the platform of the despairing effects of unrighteousness. The church throughout history has often been its strongest and most spiritually effective in the midst of hostile environments. The blood of the martyrs has often lit the flames of the Spirit. Our worst fear should not be that we would lose America, but rather that we would lose our primary passion and foundational calling to win the lost.

The Challenge

But herein lies our challenge. How do we effectively bring redemption and its life-changing power to such a decadent environment? How do we affect an environment that is often disinterested in our God and our message, distracted by material gain and affluence, and, at worst, hostile toward who we are and what we believe? In times like these, how do we change America one American at a time?

This deepening hostility toward us and our beliefs has made the Great Commission our great dilemma. Taking the gospel into all of *our* world is a far different and more difficult challenge than our forefathers faced. Yet the Washington prayer breakfast and Armitage Baptist Church give us a hint of what it takes to capture the attention not only of a disinterested world but of a world that has become disenfranchised and sometimes dead-set against Christ and Christians. It is time to rekindle the leverage of lives "so well lived" that even our enemies can't help but notice our compelling good works against which they are unable to argue.

Many of us remember our days in kindergarten. One highlight for me was storytime when Miss Bishop kept us spellbound with stories of intrigue that captured our curious minds. When we understand the biblical strategy, we will recognize that in a real sense it is storytime in the body of Christ. We now have an opportunity to live out stories of lives so well lived that they melt down the resistance and open heart doors to the miracle of redemption.

If we are to be successful in overcoming the evil of our day with the liberating message of Jesus Christ, we must first understand why the gap between the gospel and American society has not only widened but deepened in terms of resistance and, at times, open hostility. This deepening resistance to the gospel and those who carry it is a result of the dramatic changes that have taken place over the last few decades. The resistance is rooted in at least three important realities: the growing *philosophical estrangement, societal estrangement,* and our culture's obsession with an *unrestrained pursuit of pleasure.*

Philosophical Estrangement

For many generations, Americans believed in the moral law of God as the standard that determined what behaviors were acceptable, what things were right, and what was wrong. Christians and non-Christians alike generally agreed that adultery was wrong. That abortion was wrong. That it was right for men and women to marry, live together, and be faithful through their lifetime. That it was not right for men to be with men and women to be with women. It was a society where the home was held as a sacred commodity and where divorce was not only frowned upon but legally difficult. A society where, until recently, a divorced person couldn't run for president because the liability of that image would have been incompatible with cultural consensus.

Then in the mid-twentieth century a new wave of thought began to sweep through our universities and into our cultural mind-set. *Relativism* taught us that, really, there are no absolutes; there is nothing that is always right or always wrong. Relativism gave us permission to live any way we wanted to live as long as it didn't do damage to anyone else. In effect, it canceled the general agreement in our society regarding the moral law of God, erased His name from the blackboard of relevance, and kicked open the door to a whole generation of people who did not know about sin and who expressed alternative forms of behavior with no shame.

Our society has failed to heed the warning of G. K. Chesterton, who said, "Before you remove the fences, find out why they were put there in the first place."

Relativism then gave rise to *pluralism*, which basically says that everyone is entitled to his or her own truth conclusions. Since relativism said that there were no absolutes, that nothing was ever finally true, it naturally gave rise to the belief that everyone's opinion could be thought to be true. No one really had the right to stand up and say that what he or she believed about truth was the ultimate and final point of truth.

In the film version of Tom Clancy's *Clear and Present Danger*, Jack Ryan stands nearly alone as an individual who believes that there is right and there is wrong and that right is worth going to the stake for. The landscape of the story is littered with powerful people who have compromised themselves in terms of a pluralistic and pragmatic approach to both life and government. The tension between hero Jack Ryan and the rest of the characters in this story of political intrigue comes to a boiling point when Ritter, the epitome of a man without absolutes, gets in

Ryan's face and shouts, "Jack, you're a Boy Scout!" As Ryan turns and walks away Ritter yells after him, "Gray! The world is gray, Jack!"

We live in Ritter's world, where to almost everyone everything is gray. A world in which Joycelyn Elders, while serving as Surgeon General, could say to a judge as she attended her son's sentencing for his admitted dealing in cocaine, "Sir, I don't think this is a crime."[5] A world that has become so confused in its maze of relativism and pluralism that a recent ruling in New York City stated that women could ride topless on the subway without being arrested, but if they violated another rule in the subway while riding topless, such as chewing gum or smoking, they could be arrested.[6]

According to George Barna, 66 percent of Americans, both religious and nonreligious, now believe there are no absolutes. Seventy-two percent of those between the ages of eighteen and twenty-five reject the thought of absolutes.[7] In his book *The Closing of the American Mind,* the late University of Chicago professor Allan Bloom observes, "There is one thing a professor can be absolutely certain of: almost every student entering the university believes, or says he believes, that truth is relative. . . . Some are religious, some atheists; some are to the Left, some to the Right. . . . They are unified only in their relativism and in their allegiance to equality."[8]

How do we effectively communicate the absolute truth of the gospel in a society that rejects the existence of absolute truth?

The philosophical base of these thought patterns and perspectives of society makes the most fundamental tenets of sin and salvation foreign and unintelligible to the average American. Hence our dilemma. How do we proclaim a gospel that is based on the nature of sin, the violation of the absolute righteous standard of God? How do we present a gospel that not only claims that there is sin and that sin is a serious eternal problem, but that proclaims the absolute, nonpluralistic words of Christ when He declared, "I am the way, and the truth, and the life; no one comes to the Father, but through Me" (John 14:6)?

In a world where nothing is clearly wrong, a Savior is hardly necessary.

The dilemma deepens with the realization that relativism and pluralism have matured into *deconstructionism*. Deconstructionism renders reason and logic as increasingly irrelevant. According to this popular school of thought, we must deconstruct old patterns of thinking and leave in their place a void whereby people can construct life in any thought form they choose, without the checks of classical reason and logic.

This flight from reason is reflected in the new Fine Arts Center at Ohio State University which was commissioned to be built as a tribute to deconstructionist thought. The center is full of symbolic statements of the intellectual god of this day, such as columns that do not go all the way to the ceilings, stairways that do not reach the next floor, and half-finished pictures. It is dedicated to the "meaninglessness of life."

Revisionism compounds our challenge. Revisionism, the prevailing view of history in our universities and educational systems, teaches that history is unreliable. Since history was written by people prejudiced by their own perceptions and perspectives, it can't be trusted as real history. Revisionism enables us to rewrite history after our own thoughts and to recast all that has happened in the past into politically correct notions that enhance and advance the radically changed perspectives of modern man.

Think about trying to articulate the gospel into minds and hearts influenced by deconstructionist and revisionist thought, particularly in light of the fact that the gospel is grounded in both rational logic and real history.

It is consistent with classical logic to believe that the problem of mankind is related to sin, that sin offends God, and that God must judge sin. It is also logical to believe that a God who is not only just but merciful and loving would do something to reach down and help a hopelessly doomed race. It is logical to understand justice and its satisfaction at the Cross and the necessity of the empty tomb to prove that justice had been served, death had been canceled, and life could be offered. Think about presenting a gospel whose very essence is grounded in classical reason and logic to minds that no longer value logic and reason as we have known it.

Think about the challenge of witnessing regarding a historical Christ who really lived two thousand years ago, who affirmed His divinity and uniqueness through historically validated miracles that no man had ever done before or since. How does one relate the redemptive story of Golgotha, a historical place where a historical Man died on a historical cross when history is no longer regarded as reliable? And what of the historicity of this Man's resurrection, witnessed by literally hundreds of people over a season of forty days when Christ lived on earth in His other-side form?

If reason, logic, and history no longer are compelling realities in the fabric of American society, then what hope is there for the proclamation of the gospel?

This past Easter I had the privilege of proclaiming the gospel of a risen Christ in three large city churches in different areas of the country. As I prepared and delivered the message of the hope of the resurrection of Christ, I was painfully aware that many listeners would have been affected by the philosophical assumptions of our society. For them, my words, apart from some special supernatural work of the Spirit, would not only fall on disinterested ears but would be essentially unintelligible in light of how they've been conditioned to think.

Societal Estrangement

Complicating the dilemma of philosophical estrangement is the resultant *societal estrangement* that has set a dramatic distance between the message of Christ and our culture.

Gay rights, abortion, gambling, injustice, unrestraint, and immorality are all viewed by the new American mind-set as enlightenment and are celebrated as societal progress. Quite frankly, many who espouse these causes don't wake up in the morning and say, "How can I be as evil as possible today?" They simply have bought into the mind-set of a nation whose god is not the righteous God of the universe. As we have noted, our self-indulgent Americanism celebrates the rights of people to be what they want to be and do what they want to do, to have the ability to make their own personal choices without restraint or guilt. Many of these godless causes are seen as remedies to societal ills. They are viewed as a part of a new and open society where freedom and liberty finally have the right to reign.

Increasingly, our commitment to righteousness, truth, and the claims of a historical Jesus create a threat to the new agenda of our shamelessly sinful society. The biblically oriented Christian rises to say that many of these social, political agendas are not only wrong but destructive as well. We label these agendas as sinful and claim that God will ultimately hold people accountable for these actions that are so widely celebrated.

All of this makes even the most articulate Christians look as though they are impediments to social progress. Since our convictions hold truth above tolerance, we have become marginalized and discounted by a society that not only has no interest in hearing what we have to say but desires to quiet our voices as well.

That's why we are portrayed in public discourse as being the ones who are really wrong about society. In movies and in sitcoms, Christians are the lightweights, airheads, nerds, out-of-touch elements of society. Francis Schaeffer was correct when he predicted that as America continues to move toward a secular, pagan agenda, there would be a cultural backlash against those who continued to affirm righteousness and biblical truth. That day has come.

Given all the bad press and less-than-good impressions of Christians, inviting someone to become a Christian may evoke a response something like, "A Christian! Why would I ever want to be one of those?"

Unrestrained Pursuit of Pleasure

The third impediment to our capacity to change society with the gospel is America's commitment to the *unrestrained pursuit of pleasure.* The societal shift to relativism has given permission for everyone to do what he or she wants to do and to experience all kinds of pleasures without restraint. As Paul wrote to Timothy, in the end times men would become "lovers of pleasure rather than lovers of God" (2 Timothy 3:4).

How do you communicate the gospel to a pleasure-obsessed society when at the very core of the gospel is the reality that some pleasure is sinful, rendering us guilty before God, and that God calls us to repentance and a life of both discipline and self-control?

Options

In the face of a culture that is so distanced, disenfranchised, and at best disinterested in the gospel, what are our options in terms of making strides toward spiritual victories won for Christ in the fabric of America? To look at us through the last few decades, you would think that perhaps we were as confused as our culture.

As Christians stand on the rim of the arena of our society, some are waving Bibles in the air, shaking their fists in angry declarations of condemnation to those in the arena who are advocates of all that is wrong. Others stand on the rim clutching Bibles to their chests with tears running down their cheeks, moved by the plight of the lost but intimidated, unable to reach out and touch them for Christ. Some have dropped their Bibles so that as the world glances their way, they will appear to be more relevant and less threatening. Others have their ratchet kits out and are dismantling the gospel to remove from it any issues of offense that would be unpalatable to a secular society. Some are building voting booths to ballot the trouble away. Still others have turned their backs on the whole mess and stand with their faces lifted toward heaven hoping that He will come now and rescue them from this dilemma. Some have decided to dabble in the arena in order to gain accessibility and credibility, only to find that the culture has had more impact on them than they have had on society.

We should be wondering, *If this is a multiple choice quiz, isn't there one more category that says "None of the Above"?* Take heart! There is.

Strategy for Triumph

The strategy of the New Testament church, whose environment was more hostile than ours, serves as our model for triumph. In the face of the emperor's claim that he be worshiped as the god of the Roman Empire, Christians claimed that Christ was God and that their allegiance was first and foremost to Him. This basic tenet of Christianity threatened the very fabric of the Roman Empire and positioned Christians as political subversives.

Early Christians were persecuted so severely that they often had to leave homes, families, villages, and vocations to flee to other parts of the known world where they could live in safety. They were fed to lions to entertain the crowds. They were covered with pitch and tied to lampposts in Rome, then lit on fire to light the streets. Yet after three centuries of pressure, oppression, and persecution, the undaunted commitment of the early church to this New Testament strategy carried such compelling power that the more they were pressed, the quicker they expanded until finally Constantine, the emperor of Rome, embraced Christianity personally and proclaimed it to be the religion of the empire.

How do we catch the attention of our world? A world that is hostile, yet increasingly hungry, needing desperately to know the redemptive cleansing of Jesus Christ? Scripture says that it is through *lives so well lived* that a watching world cannot help but notice the compelling stories told through the outcomes of our allegiance to Him.

On a recent vacation, my wife, Martie, and I took a side trip with a group of people we had never met before. I sat next to a man who obviously has never met a stranger, and immediately he and I, an unrepentant people-person myself, struck up a conversation. To our surprise, we grew up in the same town, went to the same high school, and graduated the same year. We spent much of the conversation comparing notes regarding mutual friends and memories. In the course of that conversation he said to me, "Did you say your name was Stillwell?"

I said, "No, it's Stowell."

He said, "Oh. I know a man in northern New Jersey by the name of Stillwell."

I said, "His name wouldn't be Art Stillwell, would it?" (Art Stillwell was a part of my dad's church where I grew up; he operates a major car dealership in north Jersey.)

He said, "Yes, as a matter of fact it is! I am an attorney, and I care for his legal affairs."

He commented, "Art Stillwell is like no other client I have." When I asked what he meant, he went on to say, "Most of my clients want me to keep them out of trouble no matter what it takes. When Art Stillwell is in a difficult situation and he calls on me to unravel it, I always ask, 'Art, what do you want me to do?' and his reply is always the same: 'Do what is right.' I have no other client who responds like that."

It's hard to argue with a life so well lived.

If that attorney from northern New Jersey ever gets to heaven, it will be in part if not in whole because he had one client who was non-negotiably committed to righteousness, who refused to compromise, even in the tough times. Art's life told a com-

38

pellingly observable story. His righteousness rose like the light of a city set on a hill.

Lighting the Night

Jesus Christ told His disciples that they were the light of the world and that they had the responsibility to shine. He said, "You are the light of the world. A city set on a hill cannot be hidden. Nor do men light a lamp, and put it under the peck-measure, but on the lampstand; and it gives light to all who are in the house. Let your light shine before men in such a way that they may see your good works, and glorify your Father who is in heaven" (Matthew 5:14–16).

Note that the essence of the light penetrating the darkness is defined in verse 16 as our *good works*. Good works in the context of Scripture are not simple acts of kindness or what Boy Scouts do when they help older folks cross the street. This strategy is not a call for the wimping out of the church in some kind of goody-goody format that mellows us in the face of our society's madness. Good works in the biblical context are far more powerful, more significant, more dynamic than that.

They are, in essence, the results of unintimidated righteous living, of our unqualified submission to the lordship of Jesus Christ and His

Word in our lives. Good works emanate from our unquestioned, non-negotiated allegiance to Him and the authority of His Word. Sometimes they involve the tough stuff of refusing to cheat in the marketplace, loving our enemies, consistently loving our wives and husbands, parenting our children in such a way as to produce the appealing model of a stable and fruitful home. Our strategy at its very core relies on a life that produces observable good works which create compelling stories that can't be ignored.

Note that this strategy relates to what is *seen*, not what is *heard*. How do we witness in a world that no longer wants to hear what we have to say? Christ said in Matthew 5:16 that we should let our lives so shine as an expression of obedience that those in eyeshot will *see* a quantifiable difference. Even though they have stopped listening to us, you can count on it that they are still watching us. The text indicates that as they observe the outcomes of righteousness in our lives, they will see compelling stories they will not be able to ignore. It will indeed be hard to argue with lives so well lived. It has been well said, "It's better to light one candle than to curse the darkness."

Overcoming in the Neighborhood

The Nations Ford Baptist Church in Charlotte, North Carolina, found just the right place to plant their church so they could grow and groom a ministry for God's glory. It was a vacant Presbyterian church building on the edge of what had been a long-standing blue-collar, white area of town. In fact, the Grand Wizard of the Ku Klux Klan lived down the street as did many adherents of his sect. Given the fact that the Nations Ford Baptist Church is a body of African-American believers, the prospect of their settling into the neighborhood met with stiff resistance. The pastor, Phil Davis, could have led his church down the road of political conquest by using the ACLU to guarantee their place there. He could have opted to call the editor of the *Charlotte Observer*, allowing the power of the media to publicly intimidate the neighborhood resistance. If church leaders wanted to really put on the power play, they could have called the Advocacy Hotline at the U. S. Justice Department and gotten a federal civil rights lawyer to protect their rights. Or, they could have simply decided that this was another case of the racism that for so long in the history of our nation subjugated their people and retreated into a cocoon of deepening self-pity and bitterness toward their enemies who surrounded them in the neighborhood.

Uniquely, the people of the Nations Ford Baptist Church did something far different, far more dramatic, and far more effective—something that reflected their commitment to the lordship of Christ.

They understood that there was another option available to them—the option of submitting to Christ's command to "Love your enemies, and pray for those who persecute you" (Matthew 5:44). This is the option grounded in God's plan for penetrating hostile environments with the Good News of Jesus Christ. Realizing that the neighborhood was struggling with unemployment and encroaching poverty and that many of the residents of the area were being litigated by creditors, the church focused its attention on a ministry of compassion. Since some of the members of the congregation were legal, financial, and social service professionals, they opened an office outside of the community (to avoid causing embarrassment to their new neighbors for coming to these services) and began to give legal, social, and financial counsel and service to their new neighbors. The business persons in the church offered part-time employment opportunities to the unemployed. Over a brief period these acts of love, mercy, and grace toward their enemies melted the resistance and opened the doors of that community—not only to the Nations Ford Baptist Church but to the gospel of Jesus Christ.

Since 1988, as of this writing the church has grown from 11 to 1,500. What is most significant is that 70 percent of this church growth is made up of new believers. They have started a mission church, and they financially support seven other mission churches. The power of lives so well lived—good works in the midst of a hostile neighborhood—melted down the resistance and opened community members' hearts to the power of redemption.

Taking the Strategy Personally

I am reminded of Peter's words to believers who were facing phenomenal opposition in their day—so much that they had been dispersed throughout the known world because of their claims for Jesus Christ. These Christians had become the despised and downgraded elements of society because of their unflinching allegiance to Jesus Christ as Lord and Ruler of their lives. It was to these that Peter wrote: "Keep your behavior excellent among the Gentiles, so that in the thing in which they slander you as evildoers, they may on account of your good deeds, as they observe them, glorify God in the day of visitation" (1 Peter 2:12).

Peter clearly articulated the importance of a non-negotiated commitment to righteousness. Unfortunately, the intimidating tactics of hostile environments often erode the resolve of God's people to keep their works excellent. We often fail because of the faulty notion that perhaps we are too clean, too good, too righteous, and that if we could appear to be more loose, more relevant, more liberated, and less uptight the world would respect us and listen to our message. Nothing could be further from the truth. Christians are sometimes unnecessarily intense and overbearingly rude about some things, but in regard to those issues which go against the clear teaching of Scripture, we must stake our claim in the ground and not be moved— regardless of how we are slandered (as the early church was) or made out to be the wrong ones of our society.

It should not go unnoticed that Peter reminds these Christians that they will be slandered as "evildoers." Since they called their celebrations of the Lord's Table "love feasts," rumors abounded on the street that they were involved in sexual orgies and, since these love feasts involved sharing in the body and blood of Christ, that they had cannibalistic tendencies. The early Christians were also known as destroyers of families since those who struck an allegiance with Christ often broke with the pagan traditions of their families. And most seriously, as we have noted, they were a threat to the cohesiveness and continuity of the entire empire, as they clearly expressed their allegiance to the God of the universe rather than to Caesar. Obviously this had an unsettling effect on the political power base of Rome's hold on the world, and as a result they were often portrayed as evil elements of society.

There is a sense in which we can identify with being labeled as the evildoers in society. As we hold our society accountable for righteousness and articulate through both our voices and our voting what we believe to be right, we are increasingly seen as a threat to societal agendas that are broadly viewed as being a part of a progressive society that has finally undone itself from the shackles of its restricted, superstitious past.

Yet no matter what they say about us or how they portray us, Peter instructs us to live in such a way that they will not be able to avoid noticing the evident outcomes of righteousness in our lives, our good deeds. And when the "day of visitation" comes (which I take to mean the despairing and degrading consequences of their unrighteousness), they will note the positive outcomes of our lives that stand in contrast. Many will come to inquire what it is that makes our lives so quantifiably and beneficially different from theirs.

How do you take the gospel to a world that no longer wants to hear what we have to say? In the way that Christ and Peter outlined for us: to be so committed to the lordship of Christ and His righteousness that the good works that flow through our lives as a result of our glad obedience create compelling stories that cannot be ignored. In a world where lives are leading to outcomes of despair and hopelessness, we have the privilege of catching their interest and arousing their curiosity. When they inquire how it is that our lives are different, we will have the privilege of telling them of Christ and welcoming them to glorify God with us.

What Does It Take?

What will be required, then, to implement this strategy effectively? Peter introduces the plan by citing three critically important realities that become a road map toward realizing the power of observably different lives.

A clear sense of identity. Peter begins this section with a rousing reminder regarding our identity in Jesus Christ: "But you are a chosen race, a royal priesthood, a holy nation, a people for God's own possession" (1 Peter 2:9). When we understand our privileged identity in Jesus Christ, we will no longer feel intimidated or perceive ourselves as being a part of some underprivileged class. No one outside the scope of a relationship with Jesus Christ has an identity as privileged, precious, or powerful as those of us who are His. Our spirits will not be distracted or damaged when we keep in mind who we are both now and forever in Jesus Christ. If the culture chooses to oppose and even persecute us, their sticks and stones may indeed break our bones but their names can never hurt us. Being mindful of our identity underscores courage and confidence in the process of spiritual triumph.

As long as we know the privilege of who we really are, it won't make much difference who they say we are.

A platform for proclamation. Peter indicates that God has given us this privileged identity so that we can "proclaim the excellencies of Him who has called you out of darkness into His marvelous light" (1 Peter 2:9b). As we live out our identity and display the good works that result from our commitment to Christ, we will build platforms from which we can proclaim His excellencies. It will take a willingness for us to articulate that it indeed is Jesus Christ who has made the quantifiable difference in our lives.

A Hebrew professor of mine in seminary had an opportunity to speak of Christ when he was given too much change by a bank teller. After he left the teller and counted his money, he came back to the teller and said, "Ma'am, you've given me too much money." She counted the money, affirmed that he was right, and then said, "My, you're an honest man!" He replied, "Well, it's not that I'm an honest man, it's that Jesus Christ has changed my life."

After Bernhard Langer sank the putt on the eighteenth hole to win the coveted Master's title, he was given the green blazer that only a select few are able to wear. A national TV reporter posed, "This must be the greatest day of your life!" It happened to be Easter Sunday, and Bernhard Langer replied, "It is very special to win the greatest tournament in the world, but it is even more special to win it on Easter Sunday, the day my Lord was resurrected."

A commitment to persevering patience. Peter begins the statement of the strategy with a clear call to patience and endurance when he writes, "*Keep* your behavior excellent. . . ." This is not a five-day evangelistic crusade where thousands will come forward to glorify our Father in heaven, but rather a long-term commitment that ultimately, in God's time, verifies the reality of a living Christ, demonstrated in our lives.

When it comes to this strategy, people will not be looking for a snapshot of our lives, but for a feature-length film. For believers in the former Soviet Union it took seventy years of faithful commitment to Jesus Christ in the midst of phenomenal oppression, persecution, and martyrdom to have the story of their lives be used to lift the lid of oppression and open the gates of an atheistic empire to the Good News of Jesus Christ. Church leaders in that land have told me that in a meeting with top-level bureaucrats concerning their economy's disintegration, Gorbachev asked, "Why do we oppress the very people who do not absent themselves from work, who are not alcoholics, and who give us a good day's work?" The Russian regime found it hard to argue with lives so well lived. It was finally the moment for triumph. Finally . . . after seventy years.

For the New Testament church it took three hundred years under an oppressive government before the emperor Constantine yielded to the compelling power of lives so well lived.

Although for some of us the impact of our good works may be more immediate, for others of us the influence of our works will be replicated in our children's and grandchildren's lives, and then ultimately used to speak about the excellencies of Christ in some dramatic moment beyond our own lifetime.

The point is that we are called to be routinely faithful to the strategy of a non-negotiated, unintimidated, *persevering* obedience that produces compelling stories of lives well lived —building platforms that provide opportunities to communicate the realities of Christ.

A Point of Reference

This strategy of submitting unconditionally to God and letting Him create compelling stories that a watching world cannot ignore has a reference point in ancient Old Testament history. Did you ever wonder what prompted Rahab, the prostitute living in the pagan city of Jericho, to open her home to the spies and her heart to the God of Israel? According to her own testimony, she had been convinced that the God of the Israelites was the true and living God because of the stories that God had produced through the lives of the Israelites. She said to the spies, "I know that the Lord has given you the land, and that the terror of you has fallen on us, and that all the inhabitants of the land have melted away before you. For we have heard how the Lord dried up the water of the Red Sea before you when you came out of Egypt, and what you did to the two kings of the Amorites who were beyond the Jordan, to Sihon and Og, whom you utterly destroyed. And when we heard it, our hearts melted and no courage remained in any man any longer because of you; for the Lord your God, He is God in heaven above and on earth beneath" (Joshua 2:9–11).

Interesting, isn't it, that no preacher was sent in advance, and yet this highly fortified city on the edge of the Promised Land, which under normal circumstances would have been unconquerable, was already brought to its knees by the power of the compelling stories of the reality of the God of Israel?

There is a significant pattern for us in what took place within the walls of Jericho. In the *meltdown* stage, the resistance of a hostile culture, or even of a sinful, pagan individual, is dissipated because of the noticeably different lives of God's people. As Rahab stated, "Our hearts melted and no courage remained in any man any longer."

Following the meltdown of resistance there will be some, but not all, who will take the next step and embrace our God and glorify Him with us. Of all the people in the city whose resistance was dissipated, one was willing to step forward and count herself among the redeemed. This *miracle* stage ultimately will bring to redemption not only individual lives, but extended families, and even neighborhoods. But it always starts with one life affected by a life well lived in the power of the Spirit.

This twofold sequence is lived out in both large movements that catch the attention of the entire culture, as well as in the small moments of our own lives where we have impact in our own smaller worlds.

Cultural Dilemmas

The growing despair in a world that has sold out to the godless philosophy of relativism and that has wasted itself in the pursuit of pleasure is reaping what it has sown in terms of increasing crime, decreasing effectiveness of education, insoluble economic problems, and the rising temperatures of racial tension. Increased levels of tax dollars are poured into our macro problems, and applications of well-thought social theory and the best politics and bureaucracies that we can structure seem to do no good but rather fade in effectiveness as our problems grow more insoluble. As Christians we have the unique opportunity to craft compelling stories that demonstrate Jesus Christ as the real solution to our dilemmas and resultant despair.

Juvenile Reform

A young man from the Oak Cliff Bible Fellowship, a church in Dallas pastored by Dr. Tony Evans, got into trouble with the law. When he was ready to be taken before the judge, sentenced, and incarcerated, the church called the judge and asked if it would be possible to take responsibility for this young man for six months in order to deal with the problem in his life, remedy his attitudes, and begin to restore him to be a responsible part of his community. The judge released the potential prisoner back to the church, which placed him under the mentoring of a godly man and structured a program of restoration and recovery. In six months the church presented the offender back to the judge and gave him a report, and the judge canceled the sentence. The judge was so impressed that he asked the church if it would like to take more young men under its care. The church agreed, and today it runs a rescue operation that not only saves young men from the disastrous results of incarceration, but also restores their lives to responsible living and a guaranteed eternity.

Educational Reform

Pastor James Ford, a Moody graduate and adjunct professor on our campus, pastors the South Shore Baptist Church in Chicago. A unique outreach to the community, Impact Ministries, has evolved out of that church. Pastor Ford, along with his white counterpart, Dr. John Fuder, have led the church in meeting the needs of the community in many significant ways. In their community a large percentage of the children return home after school to empty homes with no mother or father until much later at night. The church decided to welcome these latchkey kids into their facilities where they would be tutored and nurtured through academic and recreational programs. As the church's love enveloped and embraced these young lives, the program grew until a large number of students attended regularly.

In time, attitudes began to change and the grade points of the students began to soar. Teachers and administrators in the local public school could not help but notice that there had been radical changes in the students who attended the after-school program of Impact Ministries. The principal called Pastor Arthur Lyles, who operates the program, to ask what was effecting such a dramatic change in the students in the school. Pastor Lyles told him of their program and of the reason the program was opened—the fact that Christ loves these kids and that the church members wanted to be a channel of the love of Christ in their lives. At that point the principal asked Pastor Lyles to come and speak to their school faculty.

A similar incident occurred when the director of a secular after-school program came to visit Pastor Ford. This director had received about a quarter of a million dollars in federal funding; however, getting students to attend the school program had proved difficult. The director asked Pastor Ford why it was that the church could draw so many kids to its program when the federally-funded school program had so few attenders. Pastor Ford told him that he believed it was because the church was able to create an environment in which the students could not only feel that they were loved and cared for, but where they could hear that there is a God who loves and cares for them as well.

At that point the director asked Pastor Ford if he would be willing to come and speak to the students at the public school!

A compelling story of the outcomes of righteousness that caught the attention of a world that lacked solutions for its own dilemma.

It's hard to argue with lives so well lived.

Welfare Reform

Financial adviser and counselor Larry Burkett wonders what it would be like if a church that had parishioners on the welfare rolls would go to the welfare office and inquire regarding the ways in which its people were supported by the welfare program. The church could then ask if it would be possible for the church to take over that support so that its people could get off the welfare program. He continues to query about the potential impact if the church would then take the responsibility to help restore these individuals, get them jobs, and enable them to become productive in the community again.

Ronald Sider and Heidi Rolland suggest specific ways a church program could deal with the poor. Such a program would involve welfare recipients who would choose to take part in the church program instead of government programs, with the option to return to state programs at any time.

> All participants would work, volunteer, attend school or receive job or skills training from their entrance into the program. This would include parenting, life skills, home economics training, volunteer work at non-profit agencies, or apprenticeships in local businesses. . . . Every participant would be involved in a weekly small group led by a trained person. . . . The program would develop a comprehensive, integrated mix of programs designed to meet the needs of the whole person: a medical clinic; marriage and family counseling services; child care; housing (with a long-term goal of homeownership); GED [general education development] preparation; job training (in cooperation with local businesses who help design the program and guarantee a job); and a legal clinic. Emergency needs would be met through a food pantry, utility bill assistance, and other services.[9]

What could be the effect on a world that would watch God's people taking care of, helping, and transforming their own?

Racial Reconciliation

Racial tensions have rarely been as high-pitched as they are today. You would think that with all our talk about diversity and equality the world would have shaped up and learned how to embrace one another and mingle in peace, rightly affirming the worth and value of all mankind. That simply hasn't happened. It seems that the more we talk about, educate about, and legislate about diversity, the more America looks like it's on the verge of tribal warfare.

As Christians reflect God's perspective by openly embracing all of their brothers and sisters in Christ regardless of race, class, background, or cultural orientation, our world won't be able to ignore our love for each other. Wouldn't it be wonderful for them to see that we have been successful in bringing heart-level harmony among the races and divided elements of society? In fact, observers of the early church marveled at how Christians loved one another. In a self-centered, self-serving, radically individualistic environment like America, compassion, care, and concern will tell a compelling story of the power of Christ to lift us above and beyond our inclination to prejudice.

In Chicago, I know of three ministries in particular that are having great impact for Jesus Christ in their neighborhoods because of the outpouring of good works that have opened hearts and lives to the gospel. All three are outgrowths of local churches, and all three have one leader who is black and one leader who is white. Such a statement about the power of Christ does not go unnoticed in a world that cannot seem to dissolve racial tensions.

In Our Own Worlds

The vast majority of victories, however, will take place in the smaller, quieter, less-known setting of our individual lives, where routine faithfulness will be noticed on a consistent basis in our own little worlds and in sometimes small yet significant ways.

One summer evening as friends of mine stood on their front lawn, their neighbors from across the street came over and struck up a conversation. In the course of that conversation, the neighbors asked, "We've noticed that you have something different in your family than we have in ours. What is it that makes your family so unique?" They invited their neighbors in, and, sitting around the kitchen table, told how Jesus Christ had made a difference in their home.

That night the couple from across the street received Christ as their Savior.

Bob was a successful entrepreneur in his early thirties when I met him, and the story that he told me underscored afresh the power of a life well lived. Early on he had become a self-made man and lived in a beautiful house in the country with a gorgeous wife, horses in the fields, and any car he wanted to drive. He thought he had his whole world put together until one day his wife, Mary, came home and gladly announced that she had found the answer to the gnawing emptiness in their lives. She said that a friend had led her to Jesus Christ and that she was sure this was what had been missing.

Bob responded quickly and coldly that he was shocked. He reminded Mary that religion was for the blind, the lame, and the weak—not for people like them. They had everything they needed.

Through the ensuing weeks, Bob gave Mary a hard time about her newfound faith. He ridiculed her for her commitment. He was caustic, sarcastic, and cynical. Yet he noticed that through the days, through the weeks, her life became more secure and confident, and, in fact, she was becoming a more beautiful person. Her increasing sense of meaning only compounded his sense of emptiness, which led him to seriously consider suicide on three separate occasions. Finally the power of Mary's life so struck his heart that he fell to his knees all alone in a hotel room in Dayton, Ohio, lifted his face toward heaven, and prayed, "Lord, this is Bob. If You can take me the way I am, I need what You've given to Mary."

Bob told me that story in the home of a godly doctor after church one Sunday night. Bob and Mary were deeply involved in the life and ministry of that church and today continue to make a contribution to the kingdom work of Christ. All because of one life so well lived.

In a more general sense, when Christians gladly submit to the lordship of Christ and follow the principles of His Word, there will be a noticeable exemption from the despairing health outcomes of sin in terms of venereal disease and AIDS. As we resist the seductions of greed and the endless pursuit of material goods and structure our personal economies according to biblical stewardship, we will create an interesting and curious contrast in a world full of people who are in financial bondage because they believe that greed is a means to gain and that life consists of the abundance of that which they possess.

For some of us our stories will consist of peace in the center of some storm, patience in the middle of stress, or love and concern extended all the way to our enemies—compelling stories told from lives routinely committed to unflinching faithfulness to the lordship of Christ.

May God help us as a church to be so vibrantly unique that He in our day can use us to take the power of the gospel to a world which desperately needs it, to overcome evil with good, and to be used of God as instruments to advance His kingdom.

Carl Henry, theologian and gifted Christian thinker, asks,

> Can we take a holy initiative in history? Can we once more strike an apostolic stride? Can we put an ungodly world on the defensive again? Can we show men the folly of opposing Him who has already overcome the world, of rejecting fellowship with the coming King? Will we offer civilization a realistic option, or only a warning of impending doom? Will Christianity speak only to man's fears and frustrations, or will it also fill the vacuums in his heart and crown his longings for life at its best?[10]

May our lives be so compellingly lived that people cannot help but ask us about the difference and find their longings fulfilled and life at its best in Christ.

NOTES

1. Keith A. Fournier, "The Emperor Has No Clothes," *Law and Justice*, March 1994, 1–2.

2. John Leo, "An Anti-antiabortion Rally," *U.S. News & World Report*, 21 March 1994, 22.

3. Carl F. H. Henry, *Twilight of a Great Civilization: The Drift Toward Neopaganism* (Wheaton, Ill.: Crossway, 1988), 20.

4. See Joseph Stowell, *Loving Those We'd Rather Hate* (Chicago: Moody, 1994).

5. James Jefferson, *Chicago Sun Times*, "Surgeon General: Son's Drug Sale Not a Crime." 31 August 1994, 2.

6. Carrie Dowling, "New Subway Policy Sure to Turn Heads at Turnstiles," *USA Today*, 1 September 1994, 1.

7. George Barna, *The Barna Report: What Americans Believe* (Ventura, Calif.: Regal, 1991), 83–85.

8. Allan Bloom, *The Closing of the American Mind*. (New York: Simon & Schuster, 1987), 25.

9. Ronald J. Sider and Heidi Rolland, "Correcting the Welfare Tragedy: Towards a New Model for Church/State Partnership," a paper prepared for Center of Public Justice National Conference on Public Justice & Welfare Reform, 19–20 May 1994.

10. Henry, *Twilight*, 18–19.

Moody Press, a ministry of the Moody Bible
Institute, is designed for education, evangelization,
and edification. If we may assist you in knowing
more about Christ and the Christian life,
please write us without obligation:
Moody Press, c/o MLM, Chicago, Illinois 60610.